A NEW
PLAYLIST

HEARING JESUS IN A NOISY WORLD

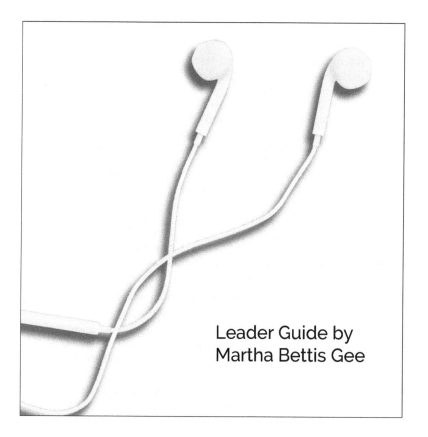

Leader Guide by
Martha Bettis Gee

JACOB ARMSTRONG

Abingdon Press
Nashville

A New Playlist:
Hearing Jesus in a Noisy World
Leader Guide

ISBN 978-1-5018-4349-5

18 19 20 21 22 23 24 25 26 27—10 9 8 7 6 5 4 3 2 1
MANUFACTURED IN THE UNITED STATES OF AMERICA

CONTENTS

TO THE LEADER

Welcome! In this study, you have the opportunity to help a group of learners explore a new playlist, one with the potential to transform our lives. The study is based on Jacob Armstrong's book, *A New Playlist: Hearing Jesus in a Noisy World*. Jacob Armstrong is founding pastor of Providence Church, a United Methodist congregation in Mt. Juliet, Tennessee. He believes that we are bombarded with words, messages, and voices that make up the playlists of our lives. More than ever before, we are distracted, anxious, and overloaded by the playlists of contemporary culture.

In contrast, this study is about a new playlist. Armstrong invites us to consider what it means, in a world with so many different messages, to listen to the song Jesus is singing. The messages in that song are the most enduring, the most truthful, and the most worthy of our attention. Armstrong asks: What would it mean to create a new playlist that allows us to hear every day what Jesus is saying?

Scripture tells us that where two or three are gathered together, we can be assured of the presence of the Holy Spirit, working in and through all those gathered. As you prepare to lead, pray for that presence and expect that you will experience it.

The study includes six sessions, and it makes use of the following components:

- the book, *A New Playlist: Hearing Jesus in a Noisy World*, by Jacob Armstrong;
- the DVD that accompanies the study;
- this Leader Guide.

Participants in the study will also need Bibles, as well as either a spiral-bound notebook for a journal or an electronic means of journaling, such as a tablet. If possible, notify those interested in the study in advance of the first session. Make arrangements for them to get copies of the book so that they can read the Introduction and chapter 1 before the first group meeting.

Using This Guide with Your Group

Because no two groups are alike, this guide has been designed to give you flexibility and choice in tailoring the sessions for your group. The session format is listed below. You may choose any or all of the activities, adapting them as you wish to meet the schedule and needs of your particular group.

The Leader Guide offers a basic session plan designed to be completed in a session of about 45 minutes in length. Select ahead of time which activities the group will do, for how long, and in what order. Depending on which activities you select, there may be special preparation needed. The leader is alerted in the session plan when advance preparation is needed.

Session Format

Planning the Session
Session Goals
Scriptural Foundation
Special Preparation

Getting Started
Opening Activity
Opening Prayer

Learning Together
   Video Study and Discussion
   Book and Bible Study and
     Discussion
   More Activities (Optional)

Wrapping Up
   Closing Activity
   Closing Prayer

Helpful Hints

Preparing for the Session

- Pray for the leading of the Holy Spirit as you prepare for the study. Pray for discernment for yourself and for each member of the study group.
- Before each session, familiarize yourself with the content. Read the book chapter again.
- Choose the session elements you will use during the group session, including the specific discussion questions you plan to cover. Be prepared, however, to adjust the session as group members interact and as questions arise. Prepare carefully, but allow space for the Holy Spirit to move in and through the group members and through you as facilitator.
- Prepare the room where the group will meet so that the space will enhance the learning process. Ideally, group members should be seated around a table or in a circle so that all can see each other. Movable chairs are best because the group will often be forming pairs or small groups for discussion.
- Bring a supply of Bibles for those who forget to bring their own. Also bring writing paper and pens for those participants who do not bring a journal or a tablet or other electronic means of journaling.
- For most sessions you will also need a chalkboard and chalk, a whiteboard and markers, or an easel with large sheets of paper and markers.

Shaping the Learning Environment

- Begin and end on time.
- Create a climate of openness, encouraging group members to participate as they feel comfortable.
- Remember that some people will jump right in with answers and comments, while others need time to process what is being discussed.
- If you notice that some group members seem never to be able to enter the conversation, ask them if they have thoughts to share. Give everyone a chance to talk, but keep the conversation moving. Moderate to prevent a few individuals from doing all the talking.
- Communicate the importance of group discussions and group exercises.
- If no one answers at first during discussions, do not be afraid of silence. Count silently to ten, then say something such as, "Would anyone like to go first?" If no one responds, venture an answer yourself and ask for comments.
- Model openness as you share with the group. Group members will follow your example. If you limit your sharing to a surface level, others will follow suit.
- Encourage multiple answers or responses before moving on.
- To help continue a discussion and give it greater depth, ask, "Why?" or "Why do you believe that?" or "Can you say more about that?"
- Affirm others' responses with comments such as "Great" or "Thanks" or "Good insight," especially if it's the first time someone has spoken during the group session.
- Monitor your own contributions. If you are doing most of the talking, back off so that you do not train the group to listen rather than speak up.
- Remember that you do not have all the answers. Your job is to keep the discussion going and encourage participation.

Managing the Session

- Honor the time schedule. If a session is running longer than expected, get consensus from the group before continuing beyond the agreed-upon ending time.
- Involve group members in various aspects of the group session, such as saying prayers or reading the Scripture.
- Note that the session guides sometimes call for breaking into smaller groups or pairs. This gives everyone a chance to speak and participate fully. Mix up the groups; don't let the same people pair up for every activity.
- As always in discussions that may involve personal sharing, confidentiality is essential. Group members should never pass along stories that have been shared in the group. Remind the group members at each session: confidentiality is crucial to the success of this study.

1.

LET IN THE LIGHT

Planning the Session

Session Goals

As a result of conversations and activities connected with this session, group members should begin to

- explore Jesus' teaching on choosing what to let in;
- encounter contrasting playlists;
- reflect on a new playlist.

Scriptural Foundation

> Now when Jesus saw the crowds, he went up on a mountainside and sat down. His disciples came to him, and he began to teach them.
>
> *(Matthew 5:1-2)*

> "The eye is the lamp of the body. If your eyes are healthy, your whole body will be full of light."
>
> *(Matthew 6:22)*

Special Preparation

- If participants are not familiar with one another, provide nametags.
- Have available a notebook or paper and pen or pencil for anyone who did not bring a notebook or an electronic device for journaling.
- On a large sheet of paper or a board, print the following from the text: "Whatever generation you belong to, you likely have a memory of music moving you and making you experience feelings in a way that was unique and memorable."
- On three large sheets of paper, print the following, one per sheet:

  » "You have to do everything."
  » "You have to say yes to everything."
  » "You have to be all places."

- Decide if you will use either of the optional activities. For creating playlists, participants will need scratch paper for jotting down entries as well as a large sheet of paper and a marker.
- For the wrapping up activity, you may want to print the group responses on a large sheet of paper or a board.
- If you decide to use a closing hymn, obtain copies of a familiar hymn such as "Open My Eyes, That I May See" or "Wonderful Words of Life," and arrange for accompaniment if needed. Versions of both with lyrics and music can be downloaded from the Internet.

Getting Started

Opening Activity

As participants arrive, welcome them to the study. Gather together. Call attention to the posted statement about the power of music from the Introduction to the book. Form pairs, and invite participants to discuss music from any genre that has moved them in a unique or memorable way. Then, back together in the large group, ask each person to introduce their partner and describe briefly what was memorable about the piece of music that the person named.

Ask someone to describe what a playlist is. Then tell the group that in this study, we will encounter the impact of the playlists with which our culture bombards us. We will examine the messages we hear and what we choose to believe about those messages. And we will reflect on how we can create a new playlist that allows us to hear what Jesus is really saying.

Opening Prayer

Pray the following prayer, or one of your own choosing:

Eternal God, we yearn to open ourselves to your Spirit so that you can speak to the deep places of our hearts. Make us more keenly aware of your presence as we seek to hear and respond to your message more fully. Amen.

Learning Together

Video Study and Discussion

In Session 1, Jacob Armstrong introduces us to the idea that today we are distracted, anxious, and overloaded by the predominant playlists of our culture—those spoken and unspoken messages that bombard us daily, seeking to convince us of what and who we should be. Armstrong, founding pastor of Providence Church, a United Methodist congregation in Mt. Juliet, Tennessee, suggests that Jesus offers us a new playlist that counters the messages of the culture.

After viewing the video segment, discuss some of the following:

- Armstrong observes that the culture's playlist has three powerful messages about who we should be and what we should do. What are they?
- He relates the story of a time when he said no to a task he had taken on in previous years. What did he say no to doing? What was his reason? What was the result?
- How does Armstrong describe his schedule? If your schedule was inscribed on a large calendar, what would it look like? What would it reveal about your priorities?
- What do you imagine that Armstrong, in being gone from home so often, was communicating to his daughter Lydia about what he valued? What do you think your own family members are learning from how you choose to spend your time?

Book and Bible Study and Discussion

Explore One of Jesus' Teachings

Invite a group member to read aloud Matthew 4:23-25.

> *Jesus went throughout Galilee, teaching in their synagogues, proclaiming the good news of the kingdom, and healing every disease and sickness among the people. News about him spread all over Syria, and people brought to him all who were ill with various diseases, those suffering severe pain, the demon-possessed, those having seizures, and the paralyzed; and he healed them. Large crowds from Galilee, the Decapolis, Jerusalem, Judea and the region across the Jordan followed him.*

Ask participants to notice that Matthew names teaching first in describing Jesus' ministry, giving us a clue that for this Gospel writer, teaching takes priority over miracles. Note that Matthew 5–7, what we call the Sermon on the Mount, is the first and longest portion of Jesus' teachings in Matthew's account. And point out that, though we call this a sermon, it could also be called the Teachings on the Mount.

Ask someone to read aloud the first foundational Scripture passage, Matthew 5:1-2.

> *Now when Jesus saw the crowds, he went up on a*
> *mountainside and sat down. His disciples came to*
> *him, and he began to teach them.*

Invite group members to quickly scan chapters 5–7, noting the headings in their Bibles that indicate the breadth and depth of Jesus' teachings in this portion of Matthew's Gospel. Then suggest that they imagine themselves to be a part of the crowd that followed Jesus.

Read aloud the second foundational Scripture, Matthew 6:22.

> *"The eye is the lamp of the body. If your eyes are*
> *healthy, your whole body will be full of light."*

Then discuss some of the following:

- Jacob Armstrong observes that although this verse addresses what we take in with our eyes, Jesus' metaphor addresses a more expansive, deeper reality. What do you think Jesus is really saying to us?
- How do you respond to Armstrong's idea that Jesus knows your heart?
- Armstrong relates the story of sitting with a friend just before the friend's death. Armstrong tells us that he can't ever recall a time in such moments when someone wanted to talk about the things they had acquired on earth or the places they had gone. What does he suggest is primarily on their minds?

Encounter Contrasting Playlists

Invite the group to refer to chapter 1 of the book, where the author suggests there is a playlist of distraction, schedule overload, and anxiety that is playing loud and clear, one that crushes our hearts. Ask one or two volunteers to summarize briefly what Armstrong tells us about the Pharisees and their understanding of the law, in contrast to how Jesus summarizes the law.

Call the group's attention to the three sheets of paper you prepared before the session, each one headed with one "playlist" that is commonly playing in our heads and influencing how we live. Point out that their discussion of the video segment touched on these playlists.

Form three small groups or pairs and assign one of the playlists to each. Ask the groups or pairs to read over the information in the chapter about their assigned playlist, as well as what the author has to say about the new playlist that can counter those messages. Suggest that participants discuss their assigned playlist, jotting down examples from their own daily lives to add to the examples the author cites.

After allowing several minutes for groups or pairs to work, invite participants to gather in the large group. Ask each pair or group to report on their conversation. Then discuss the following:

- What is the number 613 as used in this chapter? What does the author mean when he observes that it has always been hard for God's people to resist its temptation? What does the 613 keep us from focusing on?
- Which of the three playlists exerts the most influence in how you live your life? Why?
- What barriers stand in the way of our abandoning these pervasive playlists in order to open our ears and hearts to new playlists? What challenges do we face in breaking free of their influence?

Reflect on a New Playlist

Recall for the group the story that Jacob Armstrong relates about wearing glasses for the first time at the age of eight, when the negative message he had received about glasses ("Four-eyes!") was transformed by the positive message he received from his teacher. Ask them to think back on times when they experienced negative messages. Then invite the group to reflect in silence on the following questions posed in the Introduction, and then to respond in writing to one or more in their journals:

- What have you heard about yourself that you just can't shake?
- What messages of self-doubt and insecurity have you carried for years?
- What would it mean to listen to Jesus, not to the culture?

Encourage participants in the coming week to reflect on the playlists that dominate their lives. Remind them that in order to transform their lives with the new playlist that Jesus offers, they need to consider how they might open their hearts to Jesus through a deeper commitment to Scripture reading, prayer, and other spiritual practices.

More Activities (Optional)

Create a Playlist

Jacob Armstrong uses the concept of a new playlist as a metaphor for a new willingness to listen to Jesus. With this in mind, challenge participants to formulate a new playlist for themselves. Distribute scratch paper. Suggest that group members make a list of music that communicates the messages they have encountered in this chapter. It could include hymns, but also any secular music with similar messages, Scripture passages, poems, or other thoughts and insights.

After allowing time for participants to make individual lists, have them form pairs and share their lists with each other. If time allows, compile a master list of playlist entries. Participants may want to keep a running list in their journals. Encourage them to play a musical selection from their lists each day during the week, reading poems or Scriptures aloud for themselves.

Spiritual Reading of Matthew 6:22

Invite participants to engage in a spiritual reading of today's second foundational Scripture verse. Ask them to find a comfortable position for sitting and close their eyes, breathing in and out deeply several times and settling into stillness.

After an interval of silence, read Matthew 6:22 aloud once. Pause; then read it aloud slowly again. Ask group members to name aloud a word that seems to jump out to them, then to repeat that word to themselves silently. Again wait in silence; then read the verse aloud again. This time ask them to name whatever answering response was evoked to the word they identified—it might be an emotion, an image, a memory, or something else. After another time of silence, invite participants to reflect on what the meaning might be in that word and response for their lives. What might God be trying to say to them? What message might Jesus be conveying through this Scripture?

End with a time of silent prayer.

Wrapping Up

Invite those who are willing to name aloud a response to each of the following prompts from the false playlist of our culture. When everyone has had a chance to respond to a prompt, invite the group to counter that prompt by responding together with Jesus' words, our new playlist, which can be found below each prompt.

- A time when I feel pressured to do everything is when
  _____.

But Jesus says, "You are supposed to do two things: love God and love people."

- A time when I am convinced I should say yes to everything is
  _____.

But Jesus says, "Saying no is often the best yes."

- A time when I feel pressured to be all places at once is
_____.

But Jesus says, "You can be only one place."

Remind participants to read book chapter 2 before the next session.

Closing Activity

Sing or recite a familiar hymn together, such as "Open My Eyes, That I May See" or "Wonderful Words of Life."

Closing Prayer

Pray the following or a prayer of your choosing:

Amazing God, we long to listen—really listen—to Jesus. We want to let the light in, to let Jesus have our hearts. By your Spirit, open our eyes, our ears, our hearts, that we may love God and love others. Amen.

2.

WHO IS YOUR MASTER?

Planning the Session

Session Goals

As a result of conversations and activities connected with this session, group members should begin to

- explore Jesus' teaching on serving two masters;
- examine our divided hearts;
- encounter more contrasting playlists;
- reflect on a new playlist.

Scriptural Foundation

> *Now when Jesus saw the crowds, he went up on a mountainside and sat down. His disciples came to him, and he began to teach them.*
>
> *(Matthew 5:1-2)*

"No one can serve two masters. Either you will hate the one and love the other, or you will be devoted to the one and despise the other."

(Matthew 6:24)

Special Preparation

- Have available a notebook or paper and pen or pencil for anyone who did not bring a notebook or an electronic device for journaling.
- On opposite sides of your learning space, post each of the following signs:
  - » "My cell phone is often a major distraction in my daily life."
  - » "My cell phone rarely distracts me in my daily life."
- On three large sheets of paper, print the following, one per sheet:
  - » "You have to make everybody happy."
  - » "You have to look good all the time."
  - » "You have to run so fast."
- Decide if you will use any of the optional activities. For creating golden calves, you will need a variety of art materials: large sheets of paper, magazines, scissors, glue, colored markers or crayons.
- Decide if you will sing or recite the suggested hymn, "There's Something About That Name" for the closing activity. Obtain copies of the hymn and arrange for accompaniment if needed. Several versions can be found on the Internet.

Getting Started

Opening Activity

As participants arrive, welcome them to the study. Gather together. If there are newcomers who were not present for the first session, and as a way of reviewing, invite someone to read aloud Matthew 5:1-2.

Now when Jesus saw the crowds, he went up on a
mountainside and sat down. His disciples came to
him, and he began to teach them.

Remind the group that in Session 1, they explored one of Jesus'
teachings from the Sermon on the Mount. Ask a volunteer to read
aloud Matthew 6:22.

"The eye is the lamp of the body. If your eyes are
healthy, your whole body will be full of light."

Explain that the author of the study book, Jacob Armstrong, uses
this Scripture as an entry point into understanding Jesus' teachings,
messages that counter what Armstrong calls the cultural "playlists"
with which we are bombarded every day.

Invite volunteers who were present for the first session to report on
their experiences in identifying the playlists that dominate their lives
and their experiences in devoting more time to spiritual practices that
serve to open their hearts more fully to Jesus' messages.

With a show of hands, ask participants to indicate if they have their
phones with them. Acknowledging that cell phones are a necessary
element in our lives today, invite group members to indicate how much
of a distraction they are. Point out the signs you posted at opposite sides
of your learning space, and ask participants to line up on a continuum
between the two signs, placing themselves at the point that they think
indicates the degree of distraction they experience.

When everyone has found an appropriate position on the continuum,
invite one or two volunteers to describe why they placed themselves
where they did. Then tell the group members that in this session, they
will explore how cultural playlists serve to distract us from hearing the
message of Jesus.

Opening Prayer

Pray together, using the following prayer or one of your own choosing:

Gracious God, we come seeking to open our eyes, our ears, and our hearts more fully to the message of Jesus. We know we are distracted by other messages that come at us from all sides. Be with us, as you have promised, as together we encounter you in your word and in our interactions with one another. Amen.

Learning Together

Video Study and Discussion

In Session 2, we encounter the many distractions we face on a daily basis—distractions that lead to divisions. We examine the need to rid ourselves of those competing masters that threaten our commitment to our one true master, Jesus Christ. After viewing the video segment, discuss some of the following:

- Jacob Armstrong describes a time when he bought a new car. Describe what happened to that clean car. What did Armstrong discover about himself? What do you think he communicated to his three little girls? What "masters" or "little gods" can you identify in your own life?
- What important distinction about identity is Armstrong noting when he speaks of those who close big business deals, those who love a football team, or moms with a perfection complex? What aspects of your life can you name that could pose a danger to how you identify yourself? How important to you is what you do, what you own, or whom you know?

Book and Bible Study and Discussion

Explore One of Jesus' Teachings

Ask the group to quickly review what the book chapter 2 has to say about the old covenant. Then ask a volunteer to briefly summarize how the old covenant was lived out in blood sacrifices. Remind participants that in Session 1, they discovered that the old covenant involved trying to adhere to some 613 laws. Ask:

- How did Jesus summarize the Law and the Prophets? How did he transform that understanding of living up to the old covenant into a new covenant?

Point out that in this study, participants are exploring Jesus' teachings through what is called the Sermon on the Mount, found in Matthew 5–7. Ask someone to read aloud today's second foundational Scripture, Matthew 6:24.

> *"No one can serve two masters. Either you will hate the one and love the other, or you will be devoted to the one and despise the other."*

Invite group members to consider their daily lives and reflect in silence on the following question:

- What "masters" do you serve?

Then invite them to name those elements of their lives that seem to take up the bulk of their time and attention. As these are named, write them on a large sheet of paper or a board.

Examine Our Divided Hearts

The author tells us that a quotation most often attributed to Abraham Lincoln, the words "A house divided against itself cannot stand," was first spoken by Jesus. Invite a volunteer to read aloud Matthew 12:25.

And Jesus knew their thoughts, and said unto them,
Every kingdom divided against itself is brought to
desolation; and every city or house divided against
itself shall not stand. (KJV)

Ask someone to briefly summarize what the chapter tells us about distraction addiction. Discuss some of the following:

- Jacob Armstrong suggests that Jesus' message in the Sermon on the Mount is not about politics, money, prayer, following laws, or even giving to those in need. What is it about?
- What does Armstrong contend is the source of our divided hearts?
- Remind the group that in the video discussion, they considered what masters or gods they could identify in their own lives. How does the author define a god? What does he suggest the Bible has to say about distinguishing between God (big G) and gods (little g)?

Ask participants to revisit the list of "masters" the group just compiled. Suggest that they make a note in their journals of the "masters" or "little gods" they identified to which they may be giving an allegiance they owe to Jesus.

Encounter More Contrasting Playlists

We read that the main distraction is not our phones, careers, or ambition to achieve. Rather, the real distraction is letting our hearts attend to a playlist other than the word of God.

Call the group's attention to the three sheets of paper, each sheet headed with one "playlist" that is commonly playing in our heads and influencing how we live. Form three small groups or pairs, and assign one playlist to each.

Ask the groups or pairs to read over the information in the chapter about their assigned playlist, as well as what the author has to say about Jesus' new playlist that can counter those messages. Suggest that participants discuss their assigned playlist, jotting down examples from their own lives to add to the examples cited by the author.

After allowing several minutes for groups or pairs to work, invite participants to gather in the large group. Ask each pair or group to report on their conversation. Then discuss the following:

- What does the author suggest is the role of identity in moving a person from distracted and divided to open and whole?
- Where do you find your identity? In what do you place value? Is it in what you own or what you have accomplished, or do you find identity somewhere else?

Reflect on a New Playlist

Jacob Armstrong tells the story of a young boy who *loves* being an acolyte and lighting the candles in church. Ask participants what they love doing—what forms their identity—and then respond in writing to one or more of the following questions in their journals:

- How is my identity connected to my sense of purpose? Where do I find purpose?
- Do I find it essential that I answer e-mail immediately, even when it is after work hours? If so, why? How is that related to my identity and my sense of purpose?
- Do I act as if the text buzzing on my phone is more important than the person sitting in front of me? If so, why? How is that related to my identity and my sense of purpose?
- Do I numb myself in front of the television or computer instead of engaging with others in my family or circle of friends? If so, why? How is that related to my identity and my sense of purpose?

In the coming week, encourage participants to slow down, setting aside some time to be quiet so they can hear Jesus' new playlist and can remember who their master is.

More Activities (Optional)

Create More New Playlists

Remind participants that Jacob Armstrong uses the concept of a new playlist as a metaphor for a new openness and awareness to listening to Jesus. Challenge participants to add to the playlist they formulated in the last session for themselves. Suggest that they make a list of music that communicates the messages they have encountered in this chapter. It could include hymns, but also any secular music, Bible verses, poems, or other thoughts and insights.

After allowing time for participants to make individual lists, have them form pairs and share their lists. If time allows, have pairs report back to the large group. Encourage them to play a musical selection from their lists each day during the week, reading poems or Scriptures aloud for themselves.

Create "Golden Calves"

Remind the group that in Exodus, the Hebrew people created a golden calf to worship. Call attention to the list of "masters" or "little gods" the group identified, to which they may be giving allegiance they owe to Jesus. Distribute art materials. Suggest that they create visual representations of one or more of these "gods" using words, phrases, and images clipped from magazines or by drawing symbols or printing words and phrases.

After allowing time for participants to work, gather together. Invite one or more volunteers to describe what they created, or display the completed images around your learning space and invite participants to move around the space, looking at each image.

Explore More Scriptures

Split participants into two groups. Ask those in one group to read Joshua 24:1-28, and the other to read 1 Kings 18. Ask the two groups to notice moments in these Scriptures when people said no to other masters and yes to God.

Back in the large group, ask the two smaller groups to share and discuss their findings.

Wrapping Up

Remind participants of the story with which Jacob Armstrong closes chapter 2, the account of the funeral his church hosted for a neighboring church. Note that in invoking the name of Jesus, the pastor was not trying to comfort those gathered to mourn with a cliché. Rather, he was speaking a statement of faith based on the name they had all claimed. Armstrong notes that his congregation has started saying it to each other in times of need and for no reason at all. "Jesus, Jesus, Jesus, Jesus. It's gonna be all right."

Invite participants to enter into a time of silent prayer, using the two phrases as breath prayers. After settling into silence and breathing in and out deeply a few times, ask them to sit quietly as you say the words aloud, speaking the words "Jesus, Jesus, Jesus, Jesus" as they inhale, and the phrase "It's gonna be all right" as they exhale. Suggest that they may want to use the phrases as breath prayers in the coming week.

Remind participants to read chapter 3 before the next session.

Closing Activity

Sing or recite together "There's Something About That Name."

Closing Prayer

Pray the following or a prayer of your choosing:

Gracious God, we thank you for the gift of your son Jesus Christ, and for his transforming message of love. Amidst the voices of the many masters who clamor for our attention, help us to focus our sight and tune our ears to Jesus' message. Guide us as we seek to align our lives with that message. Amen.

3.

DO NOT BE AFRAID

Planning the Session

Session Goals

As a result of conversations and activities connected with this session, group members should begin to

- explore Jesus' teaching on worry;
- encounter personal fears;
- examine three questions of worry;
- reflect on implications for identity.

Scriptural Foundation

> *Now when Jesus saw the crowds, he went up on a mountainside and sat down. His disciples came to him, and he began to teach them.*
>
> *(Matthew 5:1-2)*

"Therefore I tell you, do not worry about your life, what you will eat or drink; or about your body, what you will wear. Is not life more than food, and the body more than clothes? Look at the birds of the air; they do not sow or reap or store away in barns, and yet your heavenly Father feeds them. Are you not much more valuable than they? Can any one of you by worrying add a single hour to your life?"

(Matthew 6:25-27)

Special Preparation

- Have available a notebook or paper and pen or pencil for any-one who did not bring a notebook or an electronic device for journaling.
- On a large sheet of paper or a board, print the following open-ended prompt: "I am anxious/worried about . . ." Also obtain some large self-stick notes (or index cards and tape) and pens.
- On two separate large sheets of paper, print the following:

    » "Will I have enough?"
    » "Will I do enough?"

- Post these in separate locations in your learning space, or place on tables. Have markers available.
- Decide if you will do either of the optional activities. For exploring the playlist on repeat, participants will need either copies of print concordances or access to an online concordance through their smartphones. They can also use concordances in adding to their personal playlists. For hearing the don't-worry songs, you will need equipment for viewing Internet videos, or participants can use individual smartphones.
- If you decide to sing or recite together the closing hymn, "His Eye Is on the Sparrow," obtain the lyrics and arrange for accompaniment if needed. Several versions can be downloaded from the Internet.

Getting Started

Opening Activity

As participants arrive, welcome them. Call their attention to the posted open-ended prompt, and point out the self-stick notes or index cards. Encourage participants to jot down one or more responses on separate notes and attach them somewhere on the sheet of paper.

Gather together. Invite volunteers to report on the extent to which they were able to slow down in the preceding week. Were they able to set aside some time to be quiet? What spiritual practices did they find helpful to focus on Jesus' new playlist and confirm who their true master is?

Call attention to the responses that group members posted around the open-ended prompt, and read each one aloud. Invite participants to make any observations about the responses, such as noting how many anxieties people seem to share, which ones relate to finances or health or situations in the world, and the like. Ask one or two volunteers to say more about one of the anxieties or worries they named.

Tell the group members that in this session, they will explore the messages that the culture communicates about our worries and how Jesus' playlist counters those messages.

Opening Prayer

Pray together, using the following prayer or one of your own choosing:

Loving God, there are so many circumstances in our lives that cause us worry and anxiety. Some of these we can control. Others are so complicated or unpredictable they are beyond the control of any one person or group. Gather our thoughts and fears and bring us into a calm place where we can contemplate the truth that, despite all we face, your presence is powerful and your love is sure. Amen.

Learning Together

Video Study and Discussion

In Session 3, we encounter one of the predominant underlying messages of our culture: "Be afraid." In contrast, a different message—the predominant message of both the Old and New testaments—is communicated to those who love and follow Jesus. That message is: "Do not be afraid." After viewing the video, discuss the following:

- Jacob Armstrong speaks of persons from the Old and New testaments who heard God's message, "Do not be afraid." For which two figures was a name change—or a perception about a name—part of an identity change?
- Armstrong observes that opening our ears and heart to the affirmation, "Do not be afraid," can change how we look at ourselves and how we understand who we are. He poses this question: If you really heard those words today, what would it mean for how you look at yourself? How would you respond?
- Armstrong confesses that fifteen years ago he dreamed of a perfect life, but the story his family has lived has been something different, including his struggles with anxiety, loss, and health issues. What challenges have you faced in your life that you never expected? How might the repeated message, "Do not be afraid," resonate for you?

Book and Bible Study and Discussion

Explore One of Jesus' Teachings

Ask participants to open their Bibles to Matthew 6. Review the verses the group previously explored in Sessions 1 and 2 (Matthew 6:22 and 6:24). Then ask a volunteer to read this session's second foundational Scripture, Matthew 6:25-27.

> *"Therefore I tell you, do not worry about your life,*
> *what you will eat or drink; or about your body, what*
> *you will wear. Is not life more than food, and the body*
> *more than clothes? Look at the birds of the air; they do*
> *not sow or reap or store away in barns, and yet your*
> *heavenly Father feeds them. Are you not much more*
> *valuable than they? Can any one of you by worrying*
> *add a single hour to your life?"*

Read the following statement to the group: "God will provide me with everything I need." Ask for a show of hands, first of those who strongly agree; then of those who agree; then of those who disagree; and finally of those who strongly disagree. Invite volunteers who gave each of the responses to explain their reasoning for answering as they did. Then discuss some of the following:

- In this passage, do you think Jesus' message is that God will provide us with all the stuff we want? with everything to meet our basic needs? with something else?
- How do you reconcile Jesus' words here with the millions of people in the world who lack for the most minimal basics of potable water, food to sustain life, and shelter?
- If God intends everyone to be able to sustain life, what does the Christian faith have to say about how that will come about?
- What do you think Jesus is saying about our worries?

Encounter Our Fears

Ask participants to quickly review the fears Jacob Armstrong enumerates in the chapter and in the video segment. Then ask them to revisit, from the opening activity of this session, some of the things that cause them anxiety or worry. Point out that Armstrong observes that some of the fears he cites are well founded, based on fact and real experience, while others are not well founded at all.

- Which of the fears named by Armstrong do you consider well founded? Which of the fears named by the group do you consider well founded?
- The author suggests that some of our fears may be in response to the media. What are some fears that you believe fall into that category?
- What would you say is the connection between our fears and the messages that bombard us? For example, how do you think we might be affected by messages that suggest we need to buy more and more stuff in order to feel happy and secure?

Examine Two Questions of Worry

The author invites us to consider Jesus' answers to what he identifies as the three questions of worry: Will I have enough? Will I do enough? Will I be enough?

Point out that the first two questions are displayed on two sheets of paper. Split participants into two groups, and assign one of the two questions to each group. Ask each group to read over what the chapter has to say about these two questions, looking for how Jesus answers them and what insights he brings to them. Invite each group to jot down on the large sheet of paper both their responses and any questions generated by their discussion or any further insights that arise.

After allowing a few minutes for the two groups to work, come back together and ask each group to briefly report on their discussion. If questions have arisen, discuss these together.

Reflect on Implications for Identity

Call the group's attention to the third question: Will I be enough? Remind the group that this is a question of identity, and that they explored identity in the previous session. Invite them to respond to one or more of the following in writing in their journals:

- Where do I locate my identity? Is it in where I work? in what I do? in what I have or have not accomplished?
- Does my identity reside in, or has it been shaped by, something that has happened to me, such as a wrong perpetrated against me, or a loss I have endured?
- Is the way I identify myself—or the way others see me—the cause of anxiety? If this is the case, why do I think this is so? If my identity is bound up in status in some way, what is the cost to my identity if I lose that status?
- In what ways do I embrace my identity as a child of God? How fully do I define myself with this identity?

Encourage participants to continue to ponder these questions in the coming week. As they consider those situations about which they worry and are anxious, they may want to continue using the breath prayers from Session 2, speaking the words "Jesus, Jesus, Jesus, Jesus" as they inhale, and the phrase "It's gonna be all right" as they exhale. Or they may want to use this phrase: "Jesus says, 'Do not be afraid.'"

More Activities (Optional)

Explore the Playlist on Repeat

Jacob Armstrong pinpoints the affirmation "Do not be afraid" as *the* playlist of the Old and New testaments. Ask group members to quickly scan the chapter for examples Armstrong gives us from both testaments to support this belief. Also encourage them to consider any additional biblical figures Armstrong may have mentioned in the video segment. They can use a print or online concordance to locate Scripture references about Abram, Jacob, Rachel, Mary, Zechariah, and others. Have them read some of these references and then discuss:

- How is the affirmation "Do not be afraid" an identity changer?
- How is it a legacy changer?

Add to Your Personal Playlist

Remind participants that Jacob Armstrong uses the concept of the playlist as a metaphor for a new openness and awareness to the messages Jesus calls us to hear. Challenge participants to add to the playlist they have been developing for themselves. Additions to the list might include hymns and secular music with messages about not being afraid. Participants may want to use a concordance to search for some of the many Scriptures that communicate a message of reassurance about fears. They can also add verses, poems, or other thoughts and insights.

As in previous sessions, form pairs or groups of four to share lists. Encourage participants to play a musical selection from their lists each day, reading poems or Scriptures aloud for themselves.

Hear Examples of Don't-Worry Songs

The author tells us that he has always thought of this session's foundational Scripture as Jesus' "don't-worry" song for us. Ask the group to read over what he has to say about specific songs that have a don't-worry message (such as "Three Little Birds," "Don't Worry, Be Happy," "Happy," and "Don't Worry Baby"). Play recordings of those songs from the Internet. Then discuss:

- What would you say is the difference in the don't-worry message of these songs and what the author calls Jesus' don't-worry song in Matthew?

Wrapping Up

Invite participants to retrieve the self-stick notes or index cards on which they wrote down personal worries or anxieties. Ask them to listen as you read the second foundational Scripture (Matthew 6:25-27) aloud, followed by a time of silence. Then invite them to name aloud the worries or anxieties they listed or others they may have.

When everyone has had a chance to speak, end by saying, "Hear this truth from Jesus' playlist: Do not be afraid."

Remind participants to read chapter 4 before the next session.

Closing Activity

Sing or recite together the hymn "His Eye Is on the Sparrow."

Closing Prayer

Pray the following or a prayer of your choosing:

Eternal God, we give thanks for this song of assurance coming from One in whom we place our deepest trust, your son Jesus. When we let our fears and anxieties get the best of us, make your presence known. Open our ears, that we may truly listen to Jesus' message. Through the noise of fear-inducing messages that assail us from all sides, give us the discernment to hear the song that names us as your children. Amen.

4.

RULE FOLLOWERS, RULE BREAKERS

Planning the Session

Session Goals

As a result of conversations and activities connected with this session, group members should begin to

- examine two great rules of human history;
- explore Jesus' teaching about the Golden Rule;
- encounter a different way of living;
- reflect on how to be humble.

Scriptural Foundation

> *Now when Jesus saw the crowds, he went up on a mountainside and sat down. His disciples came to him, and he began to teach them.*
>
> *(Matthew 5:1-2)*

"Who among you will give your children a stone when they ask for bread? Or give them a snake when they ask for fish? If you who are evil know how to give good gifts to your children, how much more will your heavenly Father give good things to those who ask him. Therefore, you should treat people in the same way that you want people to treat you; this is the Law and the Prophets."

(Matthew 7:9-12 CEB)

What does the LORD require of you?
To act justly and to love mercy
and to walk humbly with your God.

(Micah 6:8)

Special Preparation

- Have available a notebook or paper and pen or pencil for anyone who did not bring a notebook or an electronic device for journaling.
- On a large sheet of paper or a board, print the following from the text: "When we are humble, we live open and connected lives. When we are humble, we can admit mistakes and forgive. When we are humble, we can reflect and celebrate. When we are humble, we can release control and be lifted up."
- Decide if you will use one of the optional activities.
- This session focuses on how Jesus calls us to develop the quality of humility. For some participants, however—those who have experienced abuse or marginalization, for example—it may be more important to affirm that they are children of God. Be alert to such indications and adapt questions and discussion accordingly.

Getting Started

Opening Activity

As participants arrive, welcome them. Gather together. Invite volunteers to report on whether they used one or more breath prayers during the preceding week. Also ask for any insights participants had as they pondered the questions that were posed about their identity as children of God.

Invite group members to form two groups at opposite sides of your learning space. In one location, ask those who identify themselves as rule followers to gather. Opposite that location, ask those who identify themselves as rule breakers to gather. When everyone has had a chance to make a choice, ask one or two volunteers to describe why they characterize themselves in the way that they did.

Tell participants that in this session they will explore the one rule in Jesus' playlist that sums up all the other rules about how to act. Rule followers are drawn to the idea that there could be one great rule; rule breakers are delighted at the thought that one rule would cover them all.

Opening Prayer

Pray together, using the following prayer or one of your own:

We come together, O Holy One, to encounter you in your word. Make us aware of your presence and guide us by your Spirit as we seek to attune our ears, and our hearts, to your message of love as revealed in your son Jesus Christ. Amen.

Learning Together

Video Study and Discussion

In Session 4, we are introduced to three great rules of human history as identified in a sermon by country preacher T. B. Larimore:

the Iron Rule, the Silver Rule, and the Golden Rule. Ask volunteers to define each.

The Golden Rule, like the Great Commandment, is Jesus' rule, and it is far superior to the Iron Rule or the Silver Rule. In delving deeper into Jesus' new playlist, we encounter the prophet Micah's understanding of what God requires of us. After viewing the video, discuss the following:

- In introducing the story of the good Samaritan, Armstrong invites us to imagine a scenario in which there are two groups of people who are so divided that each despises the other. Most of them worship the same God and have a shared history, but they are not in agreement. It is a country where people with the same heritage no longer talk to each other or treat other nicely. Two parties that can no longer show kindness, respect, and love. How do you respond to this scenario, and in what ways do you identify with it?
- How do you think Jesus would respond to the above scenario, a good description of our current society? What would Micah suggest is required?
- What is your takeaway from the Parable of the Cat Purses?

Book and Bible Study and Discussion

Examine Great Rules

Form pairs. Ask one person in each pair to read over the information in the text about the Iron Rule and the other to review what is said about the Silver Rule. Ask participants to summarize to their partner what is said about their assigned rule, then to give some examples of how the two rules have played out, either from their own experience or from recent events in the nation or the world.

In the large group, ask one or two volunteers to report examples they discussed. Then discuss:

- If you had to choose, which of these two rules would you identify as being the predominant playlist in our community, nation, and world?
- Which rule do you see most often exemplified in the world of business or in other areas of work with which you are familiar?

Explore One of Jesus' Teachings

Ask a volunteer to read this foundational Scripture:

> *"Who among you will give your children a stone when they ask for bread? Or give them a snake when they ask for fish? If you who are evil know how to give good gifts to your children, how much more will your heavenly Father give good things to those who ask him. Therefore, you should treat people in the same way that you want people to treat you; this is the Law and the Prophets."*
>
> *(Matthew 7:9-12 CEB)*

Then ask someone else to read Matthew 22:37-40.

> *Jesus replied: " 'Love the Lord your God with all your heart and with all your soul and with all your mind.' This is the first and greatest commandment. And the second is like it: 'Love your neighbor as yourself.' All the Law and the Prophets hang on these two commandments."*

Discuss some of the following:

- Jacob Armstrong poses a question for us: "Which is it? Do the Law and the Prophets hinge on loving God and loving neighbor or on the Golden Rule?" How does Armstrong answer? What is your response?

Invite someone to read aloud the passage we identify as the story of the good Samaritan, Luke 10:30-35. Ask:

- Where does the author see evidence of the Iron Rule and the Silver Rule at play in this account? Where does the Golden Rule come in?
- What is surprising about the character in this account who exemplifies that rule?

Encounter a Different Way of Living

Ask someone to read aloud Micah 6:8, another of the foundational Scriptures.

> *What does the LORD require of you?*
> *To act justly and to love mercy*
> *and to walk humbly with your God.*

Extending the metaphor of the playlist, the author observes that Jesus' new playlist involves more than just listening; it involves doing. Jesus' playlist is about treating people in a way that is different from the ingrained rules of our culture.

In the Scripture, the prophet Micah asks what God requires of us. Form pairs, preferably pairing up participants with a different partner than in the previous activity. Ask each person in a pair to read over what the text says about Micah's words regarding either justice or mercy.

Reflect on How to Be Humble

Point out that Jesus is the embodiment of humility and that we can learn about what it means to be humble from Jesus' playlist. Then call attention to the posted sheet with the sentences from the text calling us to consider what humility means. Ask group members to jot down each statement in their journals. Have them quickly review what the author has to say about each statement and identify which ones represent the biggest challenge for them personally. Ask them to consider some of the following:

- Is my tendency to think too highly of myself closing me off from new relationships?
- Do I find it difficult to admit, to myself or to others, when I have made a mistake?
- Am I moving too fast to hear Jesus' voice? Am I reluctant to celebrate another's success?
- Do I find it difficult to relinquish control?

Be aware that for some in the group, the struggle may be more about seeing themselves as a child of God than about humility. Encourage these persons to consider how Jesus calls them to value themselves more fully and to embrace Jesus' affirmation of who they are.

Encourage participants to reflect on these questions in their devotional times during the coming week.

More Activities (Optional)

Experience a Role Play

Invite the group to engage in role-playing the story of the good Samaritan. Ask for volunteers to take the parts of the robbers, the priest, the Levite, and the Samaritan. Ask someone to read the story aloud in Luke 10:30-35, stopping at several points to consider the following:

- After verse 30: Ask the "robbers" to describe what they did and what motivated them to act in this way.
- After verses 31-32: Ask the "priest" and the "Levite" to respond.
- After verses 33-35: Invite the "Samaritan" to speak about his motivations.

Debrief by summarizing with the group which of the three rules were exemplified by the characters. Discuss:

- Do you think there was any risk involved for the Samaritan to act in this way? Is there ever a risk for us if we choose to follow the Golden Rule? If so, what risks are there?
- How did the Samaritan demonstrate mercy? Was justice demonstrated as well? If so, in what actions?

Explore Mercy in Jesus' Playlist

The author cites several examples of Jesus demonstrating mercy. Invite participants to read John 8:1-11, about the woman caught in adultery. Ask the group to discuss Jesus' response to the woman caught in adultery. Discuss:

- What response might persons have expected Jesus to make to this person who deserved judgment?
- What does this account tell us about how Jesus responds to us?

Continue Developing Personal Playlists

As in previous sessions, invite participants to continue developing their own personal playlists of music, poems, insights, and Scriptures related to the themes of this session.

Wrapping Up

Invite participants to review T. B. Larimore's three rules of human behavior. As you name each of the first two rules, invite participants to call out responses:

- The Iron Rule says, "Do what you are big enough to do." Where have you see this rule in operation?
- The Silver Rule says, "What you do not wish done to you, do not do to others." Where do you see this rule?

Point out that in listening to Jesus' new playlist, we are called to respond to those situations where we can counter the effects of both the Iron Rule and the Silver Rule. In doing so, we can live out the Golden Rule. Invite volunteers to name responses they might make to the examples named of the Iron Rule and Silver Rule.

Remind participants to read chapter 5 before the next session.

Closing Activity

Perhaps the first recorded song in the early church's playlist is found in Philippians. Ask participants to listen as you read this song aloud:

Christ Jesus:

> *Who, being in very nature God,*
> *did not consider equality with God something to*
> *be used to his own advantage;*
> *rather, he made himself nothing*
> *by taking the very nature of a servant,*
> *being made in human likeness.*
> *And being found in appearance as a man,*
> *he humbled himself*
> *by becoming obedient to death—*
> *even death on a cross!*
>
> *(Philippians 2:5-8)*

Closing Prayer

Pray the following or a prayer of your choosing:

Awesome God, we give thanks that as we learn to be humble, Jesus lifts us up. By your Spirit, guide our discernment as we seek to do justice and love mercy. Stir us as we try to live more fully into our calling as disciples. Amen.

5.

THE RIGHT WORDS

Planning the Session

Session Goals

As a result of conversations and activities connected with this session, group members should begin to

- explore Jesus' teaching about "name-dropping";
- encounter the power of memory verses;
- examine trusting God;
- reflect on authentic living.

Scriptural Foundation

> *Now when Jesus saw the crowds, he went up on a mountainside and sat down. His disciples came to him, and he began to teach them.*
>
> *(Matthew 5:1-2)*

*"Not everyone who says to me, 'Lord, Lord,' will enter
the kingdom of heaven, but only the one who does the
will of my Father who is in heaven."*

(Matthew 7:21)

In that day this song will be sung in the land of Judah. . . .

Yes, LORD, walking in the way of your laws,
we wait for you;
your name and renown
are the desire of our hearts.

(Isaiah 26:1a, 8)

Special Preparation

- Have available writing materials for anyone who did not bring a notebook or an electronic device for journaling.
- Decide if you will do one of the optional activities. For creating plaques, you will need 8½-by-11 sheets of drawing paper or posterboard, plus colored markers or crayons. You will need a large sheet of paper or a board and markers, as well as index cards and small sheets of paper and pens for affirming the creed.
- If you decide to do the optional activity "Experience a Creed," write the words of the Apostles' Creed on a large sheet of paper to display in front of the group.
- If you decide to sing or recite the closing hymn, "Leaning on the Everlasting Arms," get copies of the hymn and arrange for accompaniment. Several versions can be found on the Internet.

Getting Started

Opening Activity

As participants arrive, greet each person with the words "Jesus is Lord." When most of the group are present, gather together. Spend a little time with volunteers reporting on any insights they gained in reflecting during the past week on the nature of humility. Then refer participants to the first few paragraphs of book chapter 5, where the author asserts the following:

> Some words matter. Some words, spoken by the right person at the right time in the right place, can change everything.

The author gives us the example of a pastor speaking words over a couple to pronounce them married. Invite the group to give other examples of times when words do matter and can change everything, for better or for worse. Ask:

- As you arrived, why do you think I greeted each of you with the words "Jesus is Lord"?

If no one responds, tell the group that early Christians greeted one another with these words every time they met. Point out that because of this, and considering the importance of Christian community, the author adjusts his previous statement in this way:

> The right words with the same people in the same place over and over again hold great power.

Tell the group members that in this session, they will explore the relationship between belief and confession.

Opening Prayer

Pray together, using the following prayer or one of your own:

Gracious God, we sometimes use words too casually. We may say, "Jesus is Lord," without acting as if Jesus is truly the center of our lives. Other times we use the name of Jesus in ways that demean the faith we espouse. Guide us as together we seek to encounter the power of words in your Word. Amen.

Learning Together

Video Study and Discussion

In Session 5, we explore the idea that the right words with the same people in the same place over and over again hold great power. We encounter the concept of "name-dropping," discovering that it's not enough to be a Jesus name-dropper; we must listen to Jesus' words and live as disciples in accordance with what Jesus says. And we find that listening to God's word over the din of the world's noise can lead us to a new place of trust. After viewing the video, discuss the following:

- Jacob Armstrong relates how he recently returned to the place where he and his wife were married. Formerly a church, the building is now a bank. What does he tell us he experienced in that space amidst tattered carpet and peeling paint?
- Armstrong observes that old words in old places can still hold great power for today. In what ways, if at all, have you experienced this?
- He speaks about the old words contained in the confessional statements formulated by the early church. What would you say is the relationship between belief and confession? Are both essential?

Book and Bible Study and Discussion

Explore One of Jesus' Teachings

Invite someone to define *name-dropping*. Then ask a volunteer to read aloud one of the foundational Scriptures for this session, Matthew 7:21.

> *"Not everyone who says to me, 'Lord, Lord,' will enter*
> *the kingdom of heaven, but only the one who does the*
> *will of my Father who is in heaven."*

Discuss the following:

- Jacob Armstrong observes that this Scripture is a warning to those of us who are marching to the tune of a different playlist. Why?
- In what circumstances have you observed people dropping Jesus' name in a way that's empty and contrived? Can you name a time when you yourself have been guilty of doing so?
- Recall the story that closes book chapter 2, the account of the funeral that Jacob Armstrong's church hosted for a neighboring church. (If participants' memory of this story is vague, ask a volunteer to summarize it briefly.) How would you characterize the pastor's use of the refrain "Jesus, Jesus, Jesus, Jesus"? Does this seem to you like an example of name-dropping, or does it have a different function?

We read that the prophet Isaiah provides some insight into how we can avoid this kind of false name-dropping. Ask someone to read aloud Isaiah 26:1a, 8:

In that day this song will be sung in the land of Judah. . . .

> *Yes, LORD, walking in the way of your laws,*
>   *we wait for you;*
> *your name and renown*
>   *are the desire of our hearts.*

Ask the group:

- Across many millennia, what crucial distinction does Isaiah make between the song God's people sing and the playlist of his culture—and ours?
- Armstrong notes that the new playlist—listening to God's word over the din of the world's noise—leads us to a new place of trust. When and in what circumstances have you experienced this trust?

- He suggests that trust isn't about a feeling, so even when he is feeling anxious, his heart continues to trust. How do you respond? Has this been your experience? In your opinion, does this kind of trust come naturally? Why or why not?

Examine Trusting God

Ask a volunteer to read aloud Deuteronomy 6:5.

> *Love the* LORD *your God with all your heart and with all your soul and with all your strength.*

Discuss some of the following:

- Jacob Armstrong observes that when Jesus tells us that the most important thing we can do is love God, he's not talking about a feeling. What is he talking about?
- Armstrong notes that dropping God's name into a situation, even when we don't feel God's presence, is completely appropriate and acceptable and needed. How do you respond? Do you agree or disagree? Why?
- We read that achieving a deeper trust requires a "hard lean" onto God. What does this mean?

Encounter the Power of Memory Verses

Call the group's attention to the two memory verses Jacob Armstrong has relied on during times of extreme anxiety. Form two smaller groups or pairs. Assign to one group Philippians 4:6-7 and to the other Proverbs 3:5-6.

Ask the two groups to come up with a way of presenting their assigned passage with the goal of helping the other group commit the verses to memory. For example, they might use a call-response, saying a phrase and having the group repeat it; or they might build the verses by having participants repeat a phrase, then adding the next, and so forth until the whole verse is committed to memory; or they may choose any other method that makes sense, such as creating a symbol for each phrase to help prompt the words.

Allow a few minutes for the two groups to formulate their plans; then have each group help the other memorize their verse. Debrief by discussing:

- Does one or the other of these passages resonate with you? If so, which one?
- If neither seems helpful to you, can you name a passage you would like to commit to memory in order to allay anxiety or to serve to stimulate in you a deeper trust in God?
- What are some reasons for and against the concept of memory verses? What has been your experience with memory verses?

Reflect on Authentic Living

Invite the group to reflect by writing in their journals on some of the following questions:

- To what extent am I able to trust God with all my heart? Which situations have presented the biggest challenge for my trust in God?
- When have I most fully been able to lean away from my own understanding and lean toward God? What was the most helpful to me in doing so—prayer? a particular Scripture passage? the support of others? something else?
- The author suggests that doing God's will allows us to make the confession, "Lord, Lord," and have it not be an empty song. When have you most completely experienced authentic confession in the midst of seeking to be a better disciple?
- What have been your darkest nights? To what extent has trust in God been a source of strength?

Encourage group members to continue to reflect on these questions, as well as others that arise.

More Activities (Optional)

Create a Memory Passage Plaque

Invite participants to create plaques with biblical passages that speak to them of trust in God. They may want to make a plaque with one of the two passages that have been meaningful for Jacob Armstrong, or they may choose some other passage that speaks powerfully to them.

Distribute art materials and encourage participants to use different colors or sizes of print to emphasize words or phrases that are particularly meaningful. They might also embellish with symbols or line drawings. Encourage them to post the plaque somewhere like a refrigerator door, a mirror, or near a computer, where they will see it frequently.

Experience a Creed

Jacob Armstrong relates a story about a student who asked one of his seminary professors, "What if I'm having a day or season when I just don't believe part of our creeds?" The professor answered, "That's all right. We'll believe it for you."

Remind participants that in the opening activity, you greeted them with the statement "Jesus is Lord!"—one of the earliest and simplest of the creeds or confessions. Invite the group to consider one of the most widely affirmed creeds, the Apostles' Creed. Show them the sheet of paper you prepared in advance with the Apostles' Creed. Invite group members to consider each line of the creed. Then distribute index cards or small sheets of paper and invite them to jot down any part of the creed that they don't believe or about which they have uncertainty. It may be an uncertainty of the moment, or it may be a phrase of the creed that is simply problematic for them.

Emphasize that in the midst of uncertainty or even disbelief, the assembled group can still affirm their belief. Ask each person to keep their card or paper in hand as the group recites the creed together.

Continue Developing Personal Playlists

As in previous sessions, invite participants to continue developing their own personal playlists of music, poems, insights, and Scriptures related to the themes of this session.

Wrapping Up

Remind the group that in discussing how we can drop Jesus' name in a way that's not empty and contrived but that leads more people to hear his voice, Armstrong cites a passage from Isaiah. Read the passage below as a prayer, and ask the group to repeat the final line after you.

> Yes, LORD, *walking in the way of your laws,*
> *we wait for you;*
> *your name and renown*
> *are the desire of our hearts.*
>
> *(Isaiah 26:8)*

Remind the group to read the final chapter, chapter 6, before the final session.

Closing Activity

Review for the group what the text tells us about the old hymn "Leaning on the Everlasting Arms." It was written in 1887 by Anthony J. Showalter and Elisha A. Hoffman. Showalter, a music teacher in Dalton, Georgia, received a letter from one of his former students that the student's wife had died. Showalter was distraught for his beloved student. He wrote back to the student and quoted an obscure verse from Deuteronomy: "The eternal God is *thy* refuge, and underneath *are* the everlasting arms" (Deuteronomy 33:27 KJV). Based on that verse, Showalter wrote the refrain and asked Hoffman to write the stanzas. Sing or recite the hymn together.

Closing Prayer

Jacob Armstrong tells us that his daughter Phoebe and he have a ritual for school drop. They repeat a simple morning prayer that Armstrong and his wife wrote when they were first married. Pray that prayer together. It is shown here and in the book.

O God, this day we praise you for our life and we commit our lives to you. We thank you for our Lord Jesus who gives us passion and purpose. Lead us this day by your Holy Spirit to be faithful to you and faithful to each other. Forgive us of our sins and renew us to new life in you. We believe by faith that you alone will sustain us today. Hold us safe until we are together again. Amen.

6.

THE POWER OF CONNECTION

Planning the Session

Session Goals

As a result of conversations and activities connected with this session, group members should begin to

- explore Jesus' teaching about strong foundations and connections;
- examine abiding with Jesus;
- reflect on an abiding connection.

Scriptural Foundation

> *Now when Jesus saw the crowds, he went up on a mountainside and sat down. His disciples came to him, and he began to teach them.*
>
> *(Matthew 5:1-2)*

"Therefore everyone who hears these words of mine and puts them into practice is like a wise man who built his house on the rock. The rain came down, the streams rose, and the winds blew and beat against that house; yet it did not fall, because it had its foundation on the rock. But everyone who hears these words of mine and does not put them into practice is like a foolish man who built his house on sand. The rain came down, the streams rose, and the winds blew and beat against that house, and it fell with a great crash."

(Matthew 7:24-27)

Blessed is the one
    who does not walk in step with the wicked
or stand in the way that sinners take
    or sit in the company of mockers,
but whose delight is in the law of the LORD,
    and who meditates on his law day and night.
That person is like a tree planted by streams of water,
    which yields its fruit in season
and whose leaf does not wither—
    whatever they do prospers.

(Psalm 1:1-3)

Special Preparation

- Have available writing materials for anyone who did not bring a notebook or an electronic device for journaling.
- For the opening activity, you will need a ball of yarn or string. If you prefer not to do the component of the activity that uses string to physically connect the group, you could simply stand in a close circle and talk about the connections the group has.
- On each of four separate large sheets of paper, print one of the following from the book:

> » "A new playlist is less about doing and more about being."
> » "A new playlist involves pruning."
> » "A new playlist is all about loving."
> » "A new playlist is less about surviving and more about thriving."

- Decide if you will do one of the optional activities. For creating an image of the vine, you will need drawing paper and crayons or markers.
- For the closing activity, obtain copies of the hymn "How Firm a Foundation" and arrange for accompaniment if needed. There are several versions that can be downloaded from the Internet.

Getting Started

Opening Activity

As participants arrive, welcome them to this final session in the study. Gather together. Spend a few minutes on reports from volunteers about their reflections on trusting God during the past week.

Invite participants to form a circle. Then call attention to this rhetorical question posed by the author in chapter 6:

- How many of us would love to know what it feels like to be secure and to prosper?

Ask them to briefly ponder how they would respond to the following:

- In order to prosper, I think I need . . .
- To be secure, I think I need . . .

Taking the ball of string, complete one of these open-ended prompts yourself. Then, holding one end of the string, toss the ball to someone across the circle from you. Invite them to respond to one of the two prompts and, holding the string taut, toss the ball to another participant. Continue until every participant has had a chance to respond to a prompt and the string has formed a crisscrossing web.

Point out that true security comes when we attend to Jesus' words, and an important aspect of heeding Jesus' playlist is to be connected—to his words and to one another—as we consider how to respond to those words. Tell the group members that in this final session, they will explore what Jesus' playlist says about connection.

Opening Prayer

Pray together, using the following prayer or one of your own choosing:

Bring us together, O God, for we know that where two or three of us have gathered, there you have promised to be also. Open our ears and our hearts to the words of your son Jesus. By your Spirit, stir us to attend to those words in ways that connect us more deeply with you, with others, and with the world that you love. Amen.

Learning Together

Video Study and Discussion

In Session 6, we encounter the idea that nothing is more important than what our lives are built on and connected to. We dig deeper to discover the key components of connection, and we consider the dangers inherent in disconnecting from Jesus. After viewing the video, discuss some of the following:

- Jacob Armstrong describes his experience in the Future Farmers of America as a teenage soil judger. What has this experience taught him about the foundation one should choose for building a house—or a life?

- He asks: "What does it mean to build your life on rock?" What strong winds have you experienced that have buffeted your life? How would you respond?
- Armstrong describes a shortcut that he and his brother Andy took through the property of a neighboring farmer. What connection does he make between the farmer's good stewardship of the soil and the abundance he and his brother enjoyed in the ripe watermelon?
- How do you define prosperity and growth in your own life? Where does Armstrong suggest that one finds fruitfulness?

Book and Bible Study and Discussion

Explore One of Jesus' Teachings

Invite one volunteer to read aloud Matthew 7:24-27, one of Jesus' teachings from the Sermon on the Mount and one of this session's foundational Scriptures. Ask a second participant to read Psalm 1:1-3. Discuss:

- What points does the author tell us these two Scriptures are making? What is the key factor that supports prosperity, fruitfulness, and strength in our lives?

The author makes three points regarding what Jesus' playlist says about connection. Ask group members to name those three points (connection requires intentionality; connection isn't just about duty, but delight; there's no formula for connection). Jot down these points on a large sheet of paper or a board and tell the group you will revisit them later in the session.

Examine Abiding with Jesus

Invite volunteers to read two translations of John 15:5.

"I am the vine, you are the branches. Those who abide in me and I in them bear much fruit, because apart from me you can do nothing." (NRSV)

"I am the vine; you are the branches. If you remain in me and I in you, you will bear much fruit; apart from me you can do nothing." (NIV)

Call the group's attention to what the author has to say about abiding in Jesus. Ask the group:

- How would you describe the nuances of meaning with the word *abide*, as opposed to the word *remain*?
- Can you think of other words that might convey helpful but slightly different meanings?

Review Jesus' New Playlist

Call the group's attention to the four large sheets of paper headed with Armstrong's final thoughts about Jesus' new playlist. Form four smaller groups or pairs, and assign one of the thoughts to each group or pair. Ask them to read over the information in the chapter about their assigned thought and discuss together, also thinking back over insights about connections that have emerged in earlier sessions. Then ask them to formulate one question they would like the large group to discuss.

After allowing a few minutes for work, gather in the large group and address each group's questions together. If additional questions surface during the discussion, consider those as well.

Reflect on an Abiding Connection

Revisit the points the group identified about connection in the exploring activity. Ask them to reflect on the following by writing in their journals:

- How intentional am I about my connections with Jesus' teachings? my connections to others? my connections to the hurting world for which Jesus calls us to act as disciples?
- To what extent am I focused on duty? Where, if at all, do I experience delight in my life as a disciple, and what is the source of that delight? What would it look like for me to journey further from duty to delight?
- What spiritual practices am I regularly engaged in that nurture both connection and a sense of abiding with the source of life, Jesus Christ?

Remind the group that while there are risks involved in making a full commitment to Jesus' playlist, the true risk comes when we hear Jesus' words and don't put them into practice. The most dangerous thing we can do is to disconnect from Jesus. Encourage participants to commit to pursuing deeper connections with the one whose playlist brings delight and life.

More Activities (Optional)

Create an Image of the Vine

As a way of delving more deeply into the concept of connectedness, invite participants to explore the image of the vine and the branches. Give the group this background about tending vines: The worker in the vineyard prunes away any deadwood on the vine—that is, branches that are not productive or that are weak or sickly. Then the sap can flow into the healthy branches, ensuring that the vine bears more fruit.

Distribute art materials and invite participants to sketch a grapevine with a number of branches. Then ask them to reflect on the following:

- How are the branches connected to the vine? What is the relationship of one branch to the other branches?

- What would you imagine to be the effect on the plant if a branch is unproductive or unhealthy?
- What is the function of pruning? In what ways is it necessary? How, if at all, does the concept of pruning carry over to human relationships?

Ask the group to explore the metaphor of the vine and the branches, applying it to their own lives as Christians and to how they as individuals are connected to, and have an impact on, the whole plant.

Continue to Build a Playlist

If participants have been building their own playlist, invite them to add Scriptures such as the foundational Scriptures for this session and poems or writings, as well as secular music selections and hymns that speak to connectedness. If participants have kept a running playlist in their journals, invite them to report on which items in their playlist have been the source of the deepest satisfaction throughout the study. Which entries have helped them better focus on Jesus' song?

Wrapping Up

Remind participants that throughout this study, author Jacob Armstrong has urged us to consider the influence of the playlists of the culture on our lives. Invite the group to name some of the powerful messages that bombard us on a daily basis. Which are the most destructive? Which are helpful?

As a way of summarizing the study, invite participants to call out responses to, or silently reflect on, the following open-ended prompts:

- I will choose to more fully let in the messages of Jesus' playlist by
_____.
- I will seek to focus on Jesus as my true master by
_____.

- I will more fully embrace Jesus' message of "Do not be afraid" by
  _____.
- I will work to align my actions and intentions with the Golden Rule by _____.
- I will trust God's love and seek to invoke Jesus' name by
  _____.
- I will commit more fully to abiding connection by
  _____.

If participants have been developing an ongoing personal playlist, encourage them to continue to use the music, Scriptures, and poems they have identified. Also encourage them to continue to cultivate the connections they have made with other participants in order to further nurture and support one another.

Closing Activity

Sing or recite together the hymn "How Firm a Foundation."

Closing Prayer

Pray the following or a prayer of your choosing:

Loving and sustaining God, we give thanks for this time we've spent in deep connectedness, both to you and to each other. We are so grateful for Jesus' song—a song that goes straight to our hearts. Thank you, Lord, for the words we find in your Word, for the affirmation that is ours within the community of faith, and for your Spirit that speaks from the deep places of your heart to the deep places of ours. Amen.

CPSIA information can be obtained
at www.ICGtesting.com
Printed in the USA
LVHW02s2040291217
561202LV00010B/116/P